Best Self

Self-love book for Women to Boost self-esteem, discover
Formula of Happiness and inner Desires, and start living balanced
Awesome Life

Jennifer Clarke

ISBN- 9798699984473

CONTENT

Introduction

This book will carefully lead you through your fears, self-doubts, uncertainty - to the better version of you. It will help you to work on self-esteem, find out reasons for being shy and scared, provide tips and practices to start caring and loving yourself.

Every chapter is working on a particular aspect of developing self-respect, self-love, and understanding yourself better. I am providing you with exact guides and practices that will have positive effects on productivity, relaxing, planning, and understanding your future better. The book can explain to you who you are and what are your dreams when followed.

This book will become your roadmap to self-love and positive change.

Why would you need that?
Because Self-Love Is the Key to Unlocking Your Greatness.

That is a start point on the way to self-discovery, finding inner desires, and actually getting what you want.

I encourage you to read the chapters in the order provided and perform practices and exercises. This way, you will start to act from this book, and transform this approach to the real challenges and tasks on the way to your best self.

I wish you good luck, my dear reader, and patience.

Set your soul on fire!

Chapter 1. Self-esteem

Love to yourself as the only and true way to be happy

When one hears preaches, calling for humanity to love themselves, usually, the first picture coming to mind is the meeting of some cult with its participants clapping their hands as a greeting, grinning and screaming out loud: « I love you, World!».

Real love to oneself was distorted by the wave of skepticism judging people, whose only desire was to treasure themselves. The influence of conservatism, mass media, and so-called traditions for years have been telling us that love for oneself is a sign of poor egoism. Many people are falling victim to brainwashing they have undergone themselves: In the age of the mass media global coverage we constantly compare ourselves to the incomparable - and this does not spur us on, this makes us envious, sluggish, evil, resentful. Therefore, we should ask ourselves: Is high self-esteem really so wrong?

What is self-esteem?

Self-esteem shows your own attitude to yourself. Imagine that you are attending an interview with the employer sitting in front of you being your identical copy. Who are you? What are your biggest weaknesses and strengths? What makes you unique? Four questions that seem so common and simple, the ones you're bound to hear at just about any job interview are the most devious shortcut to your personality.

Self-esteem refers to a person's perception of his or her value or worth. Looking from aside, who do you see? What are the first things to catch the eye? Do you see a sincere open-minded person or an intelligent calm man? The most catching for us are usually our imperfections.

As Nathaniel Branden once said: "Of all the judgments we pass in life, none is more important than the judgment we pass on ourselves." The way we judge ourselves, the attitude to our own inner worlds affects our chances to be successful in the professional sphere, relationships, and day-to-day life.

The self-esteem functions like an internal protection system and is inseparably connected with the belief in one's own possibilities. People with healthy self-esteem are convinced that they are able to influence themselves and their environment. This faith provides strength and energy and makes it possible to overcome difficulties and challenges.

Public recognition influences self-esteem. When we do our best to achieve something, we like to be acknowledged and when our accomplishments are recognized, we feel that our hard work is worth it. Often the reasons for low self-esteem lie in childhood when one's own needs have not been met. Parents have a particularly important role to play in the development of a healthy sense of self: they are the first ones to tell that you are a valuable person who is loved. This strengthens from the inside out and makes you feel safe and confident. But the parents' dealings with the child also play a role. If there was no respectful interaction and you were ridiculed or hurt in childhood, the self-esteem is sure to be damaged. You then develop the conviction that you are just the way you are, not the perfect one. This conviction remains even as an adult.

People with low self-esteem are the hostages of their self-doubt. Their inner voice is like a strict parent who relentlessly puts more and more limits on their own child's life. If you don't believe in yourself, despite the fact that you are extremely effective, have a big heart, and great potential, the world you live in becomes a frightening and cold place. A person with low self-esteem, constantly keeps his own weaknesses and mistakes, shouldering an unbearable bundle.

Insecure people find it difficult to accept compliments and enjoy happy moments. Often, they feel uncomfortable stealing the show. They expect to be rejected by their environment, for example, they refer to a lack of feedback from friends and acquaintances and ahead of time think that they have done something wrong.

Those who have low self-esteem are subconsciously looking for evidence to prove their unworthiness. Often these people lack experiences in which they have felt successful, moments in which they have been able to realize that they actually can overcome all challenges.

Anyone who does not believe in himself and his abilities is not convinced of what he is able to achieve. Whatever he intends to do, there is no chance to succeed without a strong belief in himself. Success can also be radiated, but shine and glory always derive from the inside. This may sound like a cliché, but just look around: In fact, almost all great personalities in history have in common their self-confidence. And that was not something put in their cradle, they had to find out a way to self-improvement, and that path is open for everyone.

The following simple steps will help you improve your self-esteem.

1. Identify your negative beliefs and give them a good scolding

Have you ever thought: I'm not good, smart, beautiful enough. I don't deserve this. I'm too old for this. I could fail, you know. It's important what people think about me. I don't have a chance anyway. No one likes me. I'm a victim of my circumstances? This voice in your head trying to blame you can be convincing, can't it? The main problem with that voice is that it doesn't come out of other people's mouths. If others said something like that, you could ignore them. No, that voice comes from you, and you can't escape it. It follows each step of your way and as long as you are awake, this malicious voice comments on your behavior and your individuality.

I have good news for you, you can mute that voice. You can learn how to replace the criticizing with a constructive and positive attitude. If you do so, you will strengthen your self-esteem and confidence. All you have to do is undergo some kind of brainwashing, a positive brainwashing.

2. Identify the positive about yourself

Remember, you are unique. When identifying the positive features in yourself you combat negative thoughts telling you that you're unworthy or don't have what it takes to be successful. It is always a good idea to make a list of positive things about yourself, such as being good at art or programming.

3. Choose your surroundings wisely

People surrounding you determine your life. Let only good people be close to your inner world. You will probably agree that certain people make you feel better than others. If there are people who make you feel unconfident, not good enough, try to avoid them. If you want to become happier with yourself, you should break up relationships that drag you down.

4. Don't push yourself

No one is perfect. The illusion of absolute best is a dystopia. You don't have to be ideal every moment of your life. You don't even have to feel good about yourself all the time. Give yourself a break. We all undergo times when we feel a bit down. It's hard always to be on top. The key is not to be too hard on yourself. Be kind to yourself, and not too critical.

5. Become more assertive and learn to protect your interests

Do you live the life that others prescribe to you? Do you have to solve other people's problems? Assertiveness is the first step to the life you dream of. Do what makes you happy. Avoid what makes you unhappy. Don't let your greatest enemy grow in you. Make up your own mind about yourself, instead of taking the opinion of others. The most important commandment of self-love: Treat yourself as you would like to be treated by others.

6. Improve your physical health

The benefits of sport and fitness are enormous. Movement and physical activity are necessary for everyone. Sports are to be practiced at any age and at any time of the year. It improves blood circulation, respiration, strengthens the nervous system, increases stress resistance, helps to lose weight or get in form muscles. Balancing your diet is also an important step to improve your physical and mental health.

7. Don`t be afraid to take on challenges

Albert Einstein said, "Everybody is a genius. But if you judge a fish by its ability to climb a tree, it will live its whole life believing that it is stupid." Every person is afraid of failure. The possibility that you "mess up" or "fail" at something becomes real only if you don't believe in yourself. What will happen if you only try?

The best thing you ever can do for yourself - is to learn how to understand yourself. The good news is it is possible. The bad one - it takes much effort and quite a lot of time. Understanding your inner impulses and desires would open your mind and bring you closer you've ever been to the real you.

Self-esteem is hidden deeply in your subconsciousness, and it's not that easy to truly influence some statements and beliefs in your head. For that, you should be open to explore, learn, and not to be afraid. You should be open to cry and feel sorry for yourself, not too much though. You should be ready to work at your life interception and interception of your personality.

How to change your attitude to the past?

There are things in life we can't change. When something that used to be so firm and solid split up not just in pieces, but in millions of small, dangerously sharp splinters that can never be glued together again, there are only two options left: to stuck on the grave of the past or go on as soon as you are ready to write the next chapters of your time here on Earth.

What can you do to overcome the failures of the past?

1. Admit that you are not okay

The first step is always to abandon the fight against reality. Getting out of the cycle of lying to yourself that nothing has happened. Instead, the admission: Firstly, it's just temporary. The situation is bad, you feel bad and here and now everything looks so bad as if the end of the world is here to come. Nevertheless, a day you may consider as the worst in your life has only 24 hours. All attempts to avoid admission will only push you deeper into despair. Take in and move on!

2. Take responsibility

So as the second step, we can (and should) take full responsibility for ourselves and our lives, starting with our attitude. After all, very few situations are so horrifying, and it is up how we decide to perceive different circumstances.

3. Answer the questions

Questions are like tram lines. With each station, you come a little closer to your ultimate goal. It helps you uncover the challenges you're facing and generate appropriate solutions to those problems.

The following questions may be helpful:

What's good about this situation?

What can I learn from this experience? How can I use it in the future?

Can I really know that it is true? This question can deprive harmful and inappropriate thoughts of power. For example, "I will never be happy again!" or "What happened is certainly only a punishment I deserve!" or "I always attract bad luck!"

What can I do for myself today?

What am I grateful for?

4. Select positive words

A man applying positive thinking consciously directs his attention to the achievement of a goal. He is able to recognize the problem, assess the opportunities and resources to solve it and create a plan of action by analyzing the risks.

A single word has the power to influence genes that regulate physical and emotional stress.

If we use positive words such as "love" and "peace", we can influence how our brain works by strengthening areas in the frontal lobe and thus improving our logical thinking.

5. Move on

Time is a precious thing, and we only become aware of it when our lifetime comes to an end, but it's too late. Too many people today got stuck in the past, or live in the future. Both are simply wasting their time not allowing themselves to live in the present. You should remember that "the best" is yet to come.

Nothing happens by accident. You can also say «for everything, there is a reason». So why should you be afraid? What's happening should be happening. Enjoy today! The day you are living now only happens once in your life. Every day is precious, and the older you get, the faster time passes. You never know when you will cease to exist, so live your life to the fullest!

Affirmations

In the modern world of new technologies, trainers of self-development and rapid achievement of success by everyone around us, it is quite difficult to find something really useful. Agree, the concept of "success" has been extremely distorted recently by various "gurus" whose main goal is to make money. For some reason unknown to us, they show the really difficult aspects of life as easy, misleading most of us. And, if we need to speak as honestly as possible, it is rather difficult to blame them for this, because they would not have done this without having a demand for such "services". Psychologically, it turns out that people actively pay attention to those things that seem to be "easy" to achieve. Such a belief is extremely difficult to change, because it really lulls: people, according to their nature, are extremely lazy, and therefore it is not difficult to convince them that something can be achieved simply and without any special problems.

The affirmations that we will talk about today are no exception. Moreover, they are the subject of speculation at various pieces of training, because they are given some miraculous things, which are sometimes very surprising to hear.

In reality, affirmations are a rather complicated process, which should be dealt with in more detail. Let's start with a simple one - defining the term "affirmations". In fact, these are some kind of positive statements, the main purpose of which is to change the way of your thoughts and beliefs, tune them in a new (positive) way.

In a similar way, any phrase that you can think about yourself can reconfigure your thoughts:
- I deserve to be successful
- I feel the power to change the world
- I am open to new acquaintances

As you can see, these are the simplest phrases that, nevertheless, can change your life. It is quite reasonable that most of you now have a similar question in your head: what has to happen in order for this to work?

In order to understand such a question, you need to turn to psychoanalytic scientists, because only they can answer such a question. If you do not delve into complex concepts, then the answer will be as follows: affirmations replace destructive thoughts in the subconscious with constructive ones. It is rather difficult to say exactly how they work, because the human brain, to be honest, has probably been studied even less than the World Ocean.

But, on a subconscious level, the work of affirmations has been clear - the fact is that systematic repetitions of the same phrases gradually penetrate the subconscious, replace outdated and sometimes destructive thoughts, displacing them with new (positive) ones.

Of course, you should understand that such a practice is not a magic wand that will bring you results in just a few minutes. Do you know how long it takes for a habit to form? That's right - 21 days. So the process of improving your thoughts is like something like that. The only difference is that it all requires a lot of effort on yourself and, most importantly, requires lots of time.

Our main task is to "train" our brain to think positively, perceiving the reality around us from a positive point of view. At first, of course, it may seem rather difficult, but over time, it will become your good habit, which will bring more and more results.

All people who are just beginning their acquaintance with such practices have one more question, to get an answer to which is extremely important for future successful activity: how to correctly formulate affirmations?

Despite the fact that we said earlier that it is quite easy to do this, below we will give a few rules that you must follow in order to achieve success:

- Any affirmation must be in the affirmative form, excluding the use of the "not" particle. The matter is that the subconscious mind will perceive it as the only correct one, and therefore the result will be almost impossible to see. So for example, instead of saying to myself - "I am not poor", it would be much more correct to say - "Every day I am getting richer." It is in this way that we can fix the necessary thoughts in our subconscious.

- An affirmation phrase should motivate you to get better. In other words, it should be such that it forces you to do something in order to achieve the goal.

- Affirmations should always assume the present tense. It would be a mistake to compose something like this - "I will become a more positive person", it would be much more correct to say - "I am always in a positive mood"

- The affirmation should not include the phrase "I can". A controversial point that not everyone likes to mention, but judge for yourself, the world already knows that you can do everything. So maybe you will start doing something?)

- Affirmations should only serve the good

Of course, it is worth noting that if you do not have any thoughts at all about how your affirmations should look, then you can always turn to the professionals in this matter. These can be a variety of psychologists, scientists, psychoanalysts, and sometimes bloggers who practice this.

In order to make it easier to start your journey, below are 20 of the most common phrases, the effectiveness of which, nevertheless, has been proven by dozens of people:

- Today is the best day of my life
- I am aware and feel my strength
- I am always lucky
- Everything I do brings me success
- I am always in the right place at the right time
- I am a money magnet
- I am a strong woman/man
- I love and appreciate myself
- My body loves to be healthy
- Happiness surrounds me
- I am stress-free
- I am grateful for my healthy body
- My life energy increases every day
- Love is concentrated in my heart
- I'm as healthy as ever
- I can take care of myself
- I stand firmly on my feet
- I deserve love and respect
- I am very successful
- I control my life

These seemingly simple phrases have already changed the lives of thousands of people and continue to do it! That is why, all you need at this stage is to believe in yourself, make your own individual list (or glaze over ours), and start changing yourself. Good luck!

Your thoughts/notes

Chapter 2. The gift of thinking positive

No matter how confused you are, do not suddenly miss turned up offers and opportunities. Pay attention to your feelings: is there something you would like to try? Maybe some business that you've always dreamed of? Has anyone in the conversation mentioned a course, a teacher, or a book that is no longer getting out of your head? Take the first step towards what feels right and see where it takes you. And do it RIGHT NOW!

This saying is a good life slogan. Doing your best not to miss opportunities would definitely make your life journey exciting and unique, opening new hobbies, friends, and career opportunities. The movie "YES, MAN" is a great illustration. (Please, do not take a movie as an instruction, it's just an example of how being open to opportunities changes lives).

To be open to the new offers and ideas, your brain should be free from negative beliefs and statements. Why? Because when you do not believe anything good can happen to you, you mostly won't even see the opportunity, and just pass by. You were not looking for a good side of a situation, and you missed a good outcome you potentially could get. Does that make sense?

As it was already mentioned, the thoughts that come to our minds have tremendous influence on our lives. Along with and after working with the adequate self-esteem, it's time to rewrite our statements and some life treatments, in order to be open to new life-changing opportunities.

Forget it if you believe thinking positive is just for some optimistic people with amazing lives you'll never get. The main point is that thinking positively is a constant hard work. And you can learn it, when deciding you are able to give much effort and reach what you want.

It is true that some people have an inclination to a more optimistic thinking, and that is okay. It does not mean they do not have troubles or worries, it means they already learned how to manage it and minimise. It is not necessary they were reading books similar to this one, or attending courses on that, maybe they learned it from a parent, or teacher, or any other example. Sometimes it even happens unconsciously -- a child has positive-thinking parents, who comment on some troubles as challenges that would give them interesting experience etc., and the child overtakes that life treatment. That is amazing, but happens not that often.

There is no sense to worry now that you didn't have that experience of overtaking positive thinking from others. It's gone and you could not influence it.

What you Can influence is your current thinking, that can be changed by graduate work and reminders from yourself, and "remaking" thoughts.

You should basically catch yourself on thinking negative, and find a way not to be pessimistic in that particular situation. Such a brainstorm.

I know, sometimes you just wake up in a bad mood and feel sad. It appears to be a significant problem nowadays. To give you an example, here is the exempt from the Google trends stats for "Sadness" searches:

The Google trends for "Sadness", US for 12 months (Oct 2019 — Oct 2020)

Yet it shows the high average result (above 75 points out of 100).

And I believe that is a kind of popular correlation, and also obvious, that the number of clinical depression being diagnosed is also increasing (Robert Sapolsky's Narration on Clinical Depression).

One of the major reasons for that, besides special cases, is the lack of neurotransmitters in the brain.

Well, here are some tips that can make you less supposed to having strong disorders and anxieties. I will not promise here the magic pills and spells, because the latter does not simply exist. However, you can try setting up your day and life with positive thinking.

How thinking really influences us

As human beings or *Homo Sapiens* we are granted with highly effective and probably the most advanced central nervous system and brains in particular. Basically thinking as well as other higher cerebral activity goes from the electric and biological interaction of the neurons and substances for transmitting signals. Depending on the quantitative and qualitative characteristics of the substances in question, the one will get slightly different results.

One group is dedicated to body movements, the other will give you various moods and decisions. The thing is that such a system can be self-controlled. And while some states of organism and character demand specific chemicals to be either added or subtracted from our body, you may wonder how the other can be managed even by silly thinking of specific things. So here we come across the event of think-and-do influence that works.

The art of thinking positive

Let me acquaintance you with the concept of Anti-Fragility, that appeared brightly in recent world literature. It was introduced by Lebanese scholar Nassim Nicholas Thaleb, currently one of the most outstanding figures in risk-management and trading. He introduced the analogy for Fragile, Non-Fragile and Antifragile events, people and activities. So, opposite to fragile (harmful or unpleasant states and conditions), the Anti-Fragility means offers training and effort to make life better and easier, suffering less from such damaging consequences.

For instance, when you do physical exercise, you suppose your muscles to micro-wounds, but in the long term you gain power and strength to stand more loads or look more powerful.

Approximately the same can happen to your brain and character.

And as some people are genetically likely to be of different body types, the man can be of some type of mind as well. So there are negativists, optimists, some sort of mixed type and so on and so forth.

However, as I mentioned before, no matter the initial type of mind, you can train it like a body. You know, when the baby is born, nobody knows if he can dance or sing, it all develops with time.

Why think positive

Be honest, you do not mind why live happily, love and be loved. Thanks to biology, the aspiration to self-saving and well-being appears to be the basic instinct, to some end, the eternal law of nature. Positive thinking is analogically the basic means to acquiring better results. Inevitably, sometimes hardships and blues mood are essential. However, it proves to be logical, that when choosing the strategy, positive thinking brings more than nothing, so why not try at least once?

Training positive thinking

The brief guide for beginners: BEGIN!

Like the training, nobody starts with tons of weight on the barbell. Simple and small trifles will please you more than the disappointment when trying to handle monstrous brain activity with no results. Instead of being submissive and down because you tried to dramatically change the way you look at the situation, but it did not help, attempt at first with basic issues. In the carrot-and-stick motivation it is extremely important to enhance your wins and sometimes diminish the failures.

The key element of this lies in biology, once again. Independent of how big your success or loss can be in the beginning, the same amount of neurotransmitters are activated. The importance of positive thinking grounds on hacking the brain somehow to get it used to various circumstances. Remember, we are still Homo Sapiens, and what can be applied to our human nature, can either aid or harm. So why not help yourself, when it does not take so much, but brings a lot more?

Some more advanced techniques are also based on our neurobiology, some rely on psychocultural peculiarities. Nevertheless, your even existence can be strongly involved and changed.

Let me now tell you about **THE BENEFITS OF POSITIVE THINKING**

The way a person thinks can affect the quality of his life in different ways. The development of positive thinking improves many indicators of human life. This type of thinking affects not only personal life, but also other processes and actions.

By changing your thinking to positive, there is a great chance to make your life better. Achieve material success and build relationships with people around you.

Also, a big plus is a positive effect on human health. With a good mood, a person perceives difficult situations much easier. Such people are unusually depressed, they have a milder reaction to stressful situations.

Speaking about the advantages of positive thinking, 10 points can be noted that will improve the quality of human life.

1. Health. People who think positively simply have no time to think about various diseases. Everyone knows that self-hypnosis is a huge force that can rule. If a person does not think about the disease or, if he is already sick, is in a positive mood, then the disease quickly recedes. The psychological state has a great influence on the patient's condition.

2. *Immunity.* There has been a lot of research on the control of immunity through thinking. Subsequently, people who thought positively had a stronger immune system. And patients with negative thoughts were prone to illness, and their immunity was completely weakened.

3. *Concentration.* Positive thoughts allow a person to focus on achieving their goal and not be distracted by groundless troubles. It is easier for such people to work efficiently, while spending less effort.

4. *Self-control.* To achieve results as quickly as possible, it is important not to deviate from the task at hand. Positive thinking is an essential factor that helps a person to work smoothly.

5. *The attraction of the positive.* As many people say, a person is accompanied by the same emotions and circumstances with which he himself approaches life. With positive thinking, the right things flow into life. Even if a person has no idea about the law of attraction, this does not exempt him from accompanying failures. But the facts show that positive thoughts allow you to achieve a lot and get quick results, while negative thoughts contribute to unfortunate circumstances.

6. *Expansion of horizons.* When a person experiences some kind of malfunction, then in most cases he gets hung up on this and spends a lot of nerves and energy to resolve the situation. Thinking positively helps you see the problem from a different perspective. From this point of view, it becomes clear that this problem is not the end of the world and that you need to continue what you started. These failures only build purposefulness and self-confidence.

7. *Improving health.* Thoughts determine the state of health and help to quickly put yourself in order. It is noted that positive people tolerate diseases more easily without exposing their body to nervous breakdowns. They understand that if they set themselves up for the worst, then they will not be able to recover soon. Optimists are attentive to their condition and do not allow diseases to overcome them.

8. *Self-assessment.* Positive thinking allows a person to maintain a level of self-esteem. Such people respect the opinions of others, but also treat such opinions with caution. They respect their own opinions and respect themselves and their loved ones. They want to live with dignity, and they do everything possible for this.

9. *Abandonment of bad habits.* There is a misconception that positive thinking does not change life, improving its quality, but only makes a person relate to his life better. People with bad habits cannot make their lives better because they spend too much time on these habits. Optimists begin to think about the consequences and begin to rid themselves of the influence of bad habits.

10. *Reducing stress.* Stressful situations always unsettle a person. But only an attitude to such situations can radically change the situation. Anyone who thinks positively will identify useful things for themselves from the obstacles that have arisen and will work further. A negative person will spend a lot of energy and nerves on the trouble that has arisen and, as a result, will remain in the negative. Positivity increases resistance to stress in various issues.

I know changing the way you think is a complicated and comprehensive task. But look at all of these benefits. *Isn't it worth it?*

Your thoughts / notes

Chapter 3. Learning to understand your emotions

This chapter will introduce you to the wide range of feelings and emotions you didn't know how to express before, and teach you to manage your emotions. I would recommend you to pay much attention, and to work hard on actually understanding the information in here, as that is the basics of harmony and happiness.

Understanding emotions will help to learn about yourself, figure out the reasons for various behaviors and relationships. You are going to see what drives you and learn how to influence that.

Emotions and feelings are an incredibly comprehensive issue in psychology. Every person has a wide range of them that reflect our subjective attitude to reality and influence the interaction with others. Feelings and emotions affect our perception of various events and situations, so it is very important to understand and control them.

There is a difference between an emotion and a feeling: the former is a person's direct reaction to certain circumstances and the latter is a stable attitude towards a definite object or subject. Generally, emotions disappear quickly while feelings last for a significant time. Imagine you have found a hundred dollars – your emotions at that moment are joy, happiness, and excitement. But as soon as you get distracted from this event they are gone. On the other side, the feeling of love for your family, a sense of revulsion to enemies are constant in time, although they are also capable of changing. Another difference between emotions and feelings lies in their nature. Emotions are mostly not attached to a specific person or object while feelings tend to belong to the social sphere and relationships with other people; it is impossible to love or hate an abstract person, we feel that way only towards someone in particular.

First of all, we distinguish two large groups of emotions: positive and negative. Basically, positive emotions are a pleasant experience. We can identify them as an approving attitude towards events, objects, and impressions, which are more complex and specific than physical sensations. The scale of emotions is quite extensive, they include love, joy, satisfaction, fun, happiness, delight, and so forth. The spectrum of negative emotions is no less than a positive one, they comprise fear, anger, disgust, sadness, rage, loneliness, etc. Negative emotion is a painful experience, an unpleasant or depressed state that appears in response to an unfavorable event or action. If emotion is discouraging and demoralizing, it is negative.

There are several classifications of emotional kinds according to different criteria. They can be simple and complex or and compound. Figuratively speaking, complex emotions are composed of elementary ones: in turn, basic emotions cannot be divided into smaller components. Moreover, feelings can slow or speed up reactions, increase or decrease energy levels, and affect attitude, mindfulness, and more. By the nature of this influence, emotions are divided into sthenic that activate life processes, give us energy, and improve productivity and asthenic which are passive and, in contrast, depress us.

One more way to characterize emotion is to divide them into lower emotions which are aimed at meeting the simplest needs and instincts, for instance, eating or sleeping, and higher ones relating to intellectual, social, moral, aesthetic, and other complex issues.

Emotions and feelings do not always appear automatically, sometimes they are triggered by external circumstances. Emotions occur situationally, they are related to a certain event. Back in the 1950s, Paul McLain, an American neurophysiologist, discovered that emotions arise in special structures of the brain, which he called limbic structures. The emotional process consists of three components: experience (awareness at the mental level), physiological processes in the nervous, endocrine, respiratory and other systems of the body, as well as the "response" that is a complex of emotion expression, for example, facial expressions, laughter or crying. That is, when the body reacts to some stimulus, reactions are triggered that ultimately lead to the manifestation of emotions. But the same reactions can be triggered in other ways, such as chemicals or other body processes that involve similar metabolism ways.

There are many techniques for recognizing your emotions and the feelings of others. Psychologists highlight observation, self-report, and measurement of physiological reactions among the most popular and effective methods of recognizing emotion. The essence of the first one is monitoring your emotional state, however, this method does not guarantee accuracy in distinguishing one emotion from another since different emotions can be expressed by the same behavior. The next technique is to describe what you feel since words are very important in defining emotions. It is worth noting that a person's description of his emotions is not completely reliable as many feelings can be unconscious and a person can deliberately or unconsciously distort his experiences in a verbal report. The last method is that different emotions are accompanied by similar physiological processes - for example, the heart rate and breathing can raise both because of joy and anger.

Psychologists recommend performing one simple exercise referred to as `Mirror` to learn to recognize your emotions properly. You need to stand in front of the mirror, relax your facial muscles, and try to express different emotions: happiness, astonishment, anger, and so on. You should repeat this exercise every day and then try to show emotions with only your eyes. Another effective method is to find ten reasons for happiness during a day, rejoice and watch how your state has changed at that moment; or, vice versa, focus on unexpected stimuli such as loud sounds or bright light and try to formulate how your emotional state changes when exposed to such stimuli.

The aforementioned techniques will help to accurately determine your emotions and form the core for further work on emotion control. Staying calm and maintaining composure does not come easy to everyone but understanding your emotions is a solid basis for mastering this skill. If emotions are constantly changing, communication with others is seriously hampered and a person feels no balance and stability in life. Because people are constantly distracted by emotions, they lose the opportunity to find a deep understanding of their needs, values , and desires. One of the main rules of controlling emotions is not to react to them and do not respond to people in kind. When you are overcome with negativity, try to distance yourself from what is happening by switching to another activity or thinking about the fact that any situation in life is an experience designed to make you a stronger person. One of the foundations of managing emotions is the ability to "slow down" your psyche in time, to restrain the progress of a specific emotion. Furthermore, breathing exercises (even one simple deep breath) help to normalize the mental and physical condition.

These rules can not only lead you to the necessary and correct thoughts but become a real guide that will show you how to control emotions and not get nervous.

I know it is important to know the definitions of the feelings and emotions, to learn to identify them in your own thoughts. Let me provide some theoretical background for you here.

Alan S. Cowen and Dacher Keltner from the University of California identified 27 distinct categories of emotions.
- Admiration
- Adoration
- Aesthetic Appreciation
- Amusement
- Anxiety
- Awe
- Awkwardness
- Boredom
- Calmness
- Confusion
- Craving
- Disgust
- Empathetic pain
- Entrancement
- Envy

- Excitement
- Fear
- Horror
- Interest
- Joy
- Nostalgia
- Romance
- Sadness
- Satisfaction
- Sexual desire
- Sympathy
- Triumph

Notice, these are just categories of emotions. There are about 300 emotions in total identified at the present moment. Go over the provided list, and make sure you understand each type of emotion. Recall your memory and find an example when you felt that type of emotion yourself.

Wanna be even more involved? I want you to be familiar with all common feelings and to know how to identify what you feel on different stages and in various situations. Here we divide feelings into pleasant and unpleasant. Please read through the table:

Pleasant feelings (Part 1)

OPEN	HAPPY	ALIVE	GOOD
understanding	great	playful	calm
confident	jubilant	courageous	peaceful
reliable	joyous	energetic	at ease
easy	lucky	liberated	comfortable
amazed	fortunate	optimistic	pleased
free	delighted	provocative	encouraged
sympathetic	overjoyed	impulsive	clever
interested	gleeful	free	surprised
satisfied	thankful	frisky	content
receptive	important	animated	quiet
accepting	festive	spirited	certain
kind	ecstatic	thrilled	relaxed
	satisfied	wonderful	serene
	glad		free and easy
	cheerful		bright
	sunny		blessed
	merry		reassured
	elated		
	jubilant		

Pleasant feelings (Part 2)

LOVE	INTERESTED	POSITIVE	STRONG
loving	concerned	eager	impulsive
considerate	affected	keen	free
affectionate	fascinated	earnest	sure
sensitive	intrigued	intent	certain
tender	absorbed	anxious	rebellious
devoted	inquisitive	inspired	unique
attracted	nosy	determined	dynamic
passionate	snoopy	excited	tenacious
admiration	engrossed	enthusiastic	hardy
warm	curious	bold	secure
touched		brave	
sympathy		daring	
close		challenged	
loved		optimistic	
comforted		re-enforced	
drawn toward		confident	
		hopeful	

Unpleasant feelings (Part 1)

ANGRY	DEPRESSED	CONFUSED	HELPLESS
irritated	lousy	upset	incapable
enraged	disappointed	doubtful	alone
hostile	discouraged	uncertain	paralyzed
insulting	ashamed	indecisive	fatigued
sore	powerless	perplexed	useless
annoyed	diminished	embarrassed	inferior
upset	guilty	hesitant	vulnerable
hateful	dissatisfied	shy	empty
unpleasant	miserable	stupefied	forced
offensive	detestable	disillusioned	hesitant
bitter	repugnant	unbelieving	despair
aggressive	despicable	skeptical	frustrated
resentful	disgusting	distrustful	distressed
inflamed	abominable	misgiving	woeful
provoked	terrible	lost	pathetic
incensed	in despair	unsure	tragic
infuriated	sulky	uneasy	in a stew

Unpleasant feelings (Part 2)

INDIFFERENT	AFRAID	HURT	SAD
insensitive	fearful	crushed	tearful
dull	terrified	tormented	sorrowful
nonchalant	suspicious	deprived	pained
neutral	anxious	pained	grief
reserved	alarmed	tortured	anguish
weary	panic	dejected	desolate
bored	nervous	rejected	desperate
preoccupied	scared	injured	pessimistic
cold	worried	offended	unhappy
disinterested	frightened	afflicted	lonely
lifeless	timid	aching	grieved
	shaky	victimized	mournful
	restless	heartbroken	dismayed
	doubtful	agonized	
	threatened	appalled	
	cowardly	humiliated	
	quaking	wronged	

Mood. Practice.

Think about the mood for the day as of the cloth you choose in the closet:

You take a hanger with a dress or a shirt, you go to the mirror, and try it on. You think about how you want to look today.

Try the same with the mood: you wake up in the morning, and try to realise what kind of person you want to be today, what you want to feel, what impression you want to make on other people. Smile and make a conscious decision.

Do that tomorrow morning. You even do not need to believe it works. All you need to do is to Try. Here: take your phone and make a reminder for tomorrow morning : "Choose a mood". Do that in the bed, while drinking coffee, or putting cloth on. Try to notice if you stick to it during the day, and in the evening estimate how good you were. Stay patient and do that every morning during the 2 weeks, and I swear, you will see the difference.

When you actually see the difference, please take 2 minutes and write a comment to the book on Amazon, letting me know it works for you. Thanks! :)

"It's too simple to be true." I've heard it soo many times. But it IS simple. You should Decide to be happy. You should be absolutely sure you deserve to be happy. You are the only person who can actually change your mood, and make you happy in the end. See? So simple, but hard at the same time.

Here is one more very useful practice I recommend you all to think about and be involved in your life.

I am pretty sure you have already heard something about "magic morning" and the importance of starting the day right. Hearing about something, thinking, or even planning is not the same as practicing, unfortunately. In this book, I am not gonna make you wake up at 5 am (or any other particular time), not gonna tell you exactly what to do and in which order. I will give you general advice and my own example of pleasant and full of energy in the morning (not a to-do list, just one of various ideas).

Let me present an example first, and insights and outputs after.

My Morning Routine

I wanna share with you, my dear readers, my personal, verified on practice, tutorial on how to make your day Better, how to live the next day deliberately and get pleasure, getting things done.

The best thing is to start from the night before. It's simple and won't take much time. Let's say you are in bed and ready to fall asleep: close your eyes and try to imagine the next day. Be realistic here, but make an effort to add as many smiles, pleasant moments and happiness as possible. Keep in mind things that are to be done tomorrow, And free of duties time you have. Wonderful if you can go step by step and imagine every activity focusing on details, people and tastes, smells. Now you can sleep.

In the morning your task is to find 10-15 minutes when nobody disturbs you -- when having big family or work early morning the good way is to wake up 15 minutes earlier. (Trust me, it's worth it). So you wake up, wash your face/brush teeth, and then go to some place (a balcony, backyard, cozy windowsill, square near your house), sit comfortably, and tune in for the day. You can come up with your own ritual, morning routine, that makes you feel good and includes things you love.

Here is my example: I wake up 25 minutes before sunrise, slide down from my bed, put on the first I see, and go to the kitchen -- to make coffee.

Cooking coffee is a small separate ritual for me: I turn on optimistic music, take a coffee package, turn on the stove (I use a turkey type coffee maker), and completely wake up until the coffee is made. I focus on the smell, blend milk, put it into my travel cup, add coffee itself, and go to the parking roof to watch the sunrise. I enjoy the view, and start mentally preparing for the upcoming day. I think about how to optimize the time, the sequence of my tasks and making a "not to forget" list. Then I take my favorite blanket and seat on the grass in a quiet place under the trees: that's the time for meditation. Mostly I meditate with classical music in the morning (Try Oliver Schuster and Ludovico Einaudi).

This morning is filled with love. First of all, to myself -- because I do things I love, the ones that inspire me. And just like that -- I settled a particular mood for the day. Yes, I made an effort to wake up and start my routine, yes, sometimes I feel lazy and unmotivated, but as soon as I slide down from my bed - I feel proud. That is the most out of morning you can get -- to feel good about yourself. That way, there is a much higher chance your day will be productive, And pleasant.

You can try different approaches and come up with your own perfect routine. It should not start at 7 am -- whenever it works for you. The main rule is to do things you love, organise your thoughts, and fill yourself with energy (this way, watching shows in the morning wouldn't work: you may like it, but id does not make you feel better).

Listen to your favorite music, take a walk, go for a run, ride a bike, do stretching, cook a family breakfast, take a shower and make a facemask, meditate -- whatever, but after that you should feel fulfilled, have much energy, and Smile.

Promise?

Morning routine advice for Beginners

Let's come up with certain "rules", more like a guideline so that you can write down and apply your own ideal morning.

1.   The main goal is to get ready for the day (whatever the day is - working/busy, or relaxing). You need to spend this time to organize your thoughts, imagine the best version of this particular day, balancing the work and the rest, useful things and pleasant things. After doing this practice on a regular basis for a while, you'll learn how to put realistic expectations and not to require too much from yourself.

2.   Secondly, your task is to make, create the mood for the whole day. Thinking positive, dreaming for a little bit, listening to favorite music, cooking favorite drink (not alcohol preferably, but various mornings happen).

3.   Find a spot of something beautiful - anything you like to look at. My ideal spot to spend morning at - is ocean shore, but until the time I can be there every morning - I have sunrises, a park close to the house, a pond, my special bench under the tree. It is not even necessary that you do the exact same things every morning. You may have a set of them, and should know that's something that feels you with strength and energy.

4.   Timing -- 20 minutes to 1 hour I'd say. It may differ for working days and days-off. Let's say you love doing some face procedures in front of the mirror listening to music and dancing. You may not have enough time to make the whole list every morning, but you can do that on Sunday for the whole hour.

5.   You should ENJOY. Just enjoy. Whatever it is. I strongly recommend to get outside during your magic morning time. Although different days may occur, and when it rains hard outside -- let's say you just stay in bed and read a fiction book, having cacao right by you. Sounds good, huh? Definitely better, than being depressed and angry because of the weather.

Everybody has difficulties and moments in life when he is too busy. Your task is not to spoil that small amount of time you can get, and use it to fill yourself with a resource, instead of rewatching stupid show for the third time.

6.   Make a list of what you like generally to define your morning routine. Then think about what things can be done in 15-50 minutes, and make an order. In the morning you should have a strict guide you should follow. Especially, in the beginning

7.   You may also do similar staff in the evening before going to bed, you can test. Based on my practice, morning works better for most of the people.

Pleasant VS Meaningful

Everybody wants to be happy, Everybody wants so that his life matters. Let me tell you something -- it depends on you. Let's go deeper and explain why these two things are so important to human beings, and why we suffer when one of them is missing.

Basically, we have 2 types of emotions -- positive and negative. They can either be preconceived, or unconditioned.

We can make such tables to visualize the feelings we have in 4 types of situations.

EMOTIONS	Positive	Negative
Unconditioned	Content, calm	Sad, depressed
Preconceived	Joyful, thrilled	Worried, angry

What does it mean?

Well, here is what you need to learn -- a human being is happy, when he either considers his actions meaningful, or is doing pleasant things.

Although, it is not enough just to enjoy life without doing anything important, or, on the contrary, to devote life to changing the world, and forget about his own feelings.

The secret of happiness lays in the right balancing of doing meaningful things, and pleasant. (Paul Dolan Concept)

Happiness = Meaningfulness + Pleasure

Let's say the firefighter suffers physically, when rescuing people, but at the same time he realizes he is doing a very important thing, and that is why he feels good.

A famous writer needs to apply strict self-discipline to finish a book (because his fans are waiting), instead of going to a beach with family -- she wants to get some pleasure of swimming and spending time with her family, feels worried she stays at home, but the feeling of meaningfulness wins at that moment, and in the end of the day she feels joyful she moved closer to the book release.

If the firefighter or the writer in these stories were just doing meaningful things and did not allow themselves to take a rest, to get some pleasure, they would not be that productive, and in the end would not enjoy the work. They need to balance.

At the same time, let's say a housewife has a glamorous life, her husband earns good money and she can do many pleasant things during the working days, since she does not have a job. Although, at some point she starts feeling depressed, as she starts to realise she wastes her life and does not leave anything meaningful after herself. She does not help people in any way, does not have her own children to raise, does not contribute to science, technology progress and so on.

It is always easier to realise what pleasant things you can do to make you feel good. The challenging task is to find what brings you joy from meaningfulness.

There is not an exact formula or checklist how to find a sense of life, since it varies a lot for different people. The only advice I can give you is to try as many things as possible -- volunteering, social organisations, working due to our major for companies that have similar values as you do, traveling.

You will be getting that understanding gradually, and in the end will find all pieces of puzzle and have the whole picture.

Your thoughts / notes

Chapter 4. Meditation

Living in the past, overthinking what happened before, living in expectations, waiting for a better time - everybody's been there.

It's natural for human beings not to be in the moment, that's what differs us from animals - the ability to plan life and think ahead. Along with that we often forget to pay attention to what's going on around. No, really! We get so involved in what's going on in our head, that we forget to see life Now, real life !

The problem here is that we never know if the future will be exactly like we were dreaming/planning, and will it be at all. And we cannot change the past, nor live it again. All you Can do is to change something at this current moment. To make an action, to open your eyes and see a squirrel running across the street, a bird sitting on your car, to hear the wind and sound of the water. Right now, not later. You need to make an effort. Make yourself pay attention. Ask "What do we see? Do I like it ? Why? What do I feel?"

Meditations help a lot in understanding yourself, that's like a particular time in your hectic schedule devoted to your inner, time to stop and notice what's going on with You, how you feel.

To slow down, relax and prepare for further challenges, to be in the moment.
To calm down, free up your mind.

I would also mention the benefits of meditation for nerves, and the brain.

❏   Meditations reduce the level of stress

Accumulated stress is one of the common reasons why a person starts meditating. Human nature has a feature of a particular reaction on danger, called "fight, or run". At that moment the body gets a sharp hormone jump, that could lead to sleep problems, depression, increasing of body pressure, getting tired quickly and a mess in mind.

Meditations help to keep the mind clear even in stressful situations and consciously choose the behavior and plan actions.

❏   Meditations increase attentiveness and help to be concentrated longer

The modern world presents an endless stream of information, and the human brains are often unable to proceed with all information and pay attention to everything that passes by. This is why it is important to learn how to separate the information you need from the information flow. People get so tired from constant information coming from everywhere, that they need a Break. Meditations are a great way to give your brain a rest every day, while improving concentration and having a mental silence.

❑ Meditations help to control anxiousness

Human brain has a section responsible for fears. It works similar to a radar that looks for sources of danger. Sometimes it gives the human a false signal (based on associations or bad memories) and causes unreasonable anxiety. That process is unconscious, and it is hard to control it mentally. But meditations can reduce the anxiety and make a calming effect on the person, when performed right.

❑ Meditations help to actually realise what is going on

Meditations keep you in the current moment, making you focus on your feelings and life. That increases consciousness and the effect keeps when you stand up and go to solve your problems, meet with parents, do sports and so on. Meditations bring you to the real moment every day.

❑ Meditations contribute to emotional health

Our brain "likes" to focus on unpleasant situations and to transfer that state to other aspects of life. Let's say you have a conflict at work. The brain works in that way that it transfers work problems to a family or relationship, and you do not realise it. People practicing meditations can better control thoughts and emotions, and do not have tha problem. While meditating, special neuron connections appear, that develop an ability to rationally estimate problems.

❑ Meditations contribute to a better sleeping
Since meditations unload your brain and calm down, many people observe better sleeping and feeling more energy after waking up. That way, we fall asleep faster, and the quality of sleep is higher.

❑ Meditations prevent brain aging
It is scientifically proved that meditations prevent brain aging by creating new neuron connections and launching brain activity. That saves you from forgetting basic things in the future, and serves as a pleasant exercise, having multiple positive influences.

You need meditations if ..

-       you do not trust. Yourself, people. If you have issues with self esteem, you are often jealous and feeling bad

-       you have this feeling that everything goes wrong, and you cannot explain why wrong, how should it go

-       you are criticizing, or are criticized often

-       you do not feel like you have a balanced and saturated life

-       you have problems with concentrating your attention on one task

-       you get irritated easily

-       you are being manipulated

In case my arguments persuaded you to try meditations, I recommend you to start from testing different types of them and seeing which ones have the best effect.

There are three main types of meditation and many practices based on them:
• meditation to calm the mind (Skt. Shamatha), concentration of attention on breath, sounds or images;
• mindfulness meditation (Skt. Vipashyana, better known as vipassana), expansion of attention and simultaneous perception of oneself and the outside world;
• meditation of loving kindness (Skt. Maitri), directing attention on a kind attitude towards oneself, on love for living beings, etc.

1. Breath meditation

This meditation leads to calmness, trains focus and concentration of attention, and helps to move away from disturbing thoughts.

DURATION
You can start this practice with 3-5 minutes,
gradually increase to 10-15 minutes.

REGULARITY
Meditate daily, 1-2 times a day.

1. Get into the correct posture.

This practice can be done both sitting and lying down. You can put a rug or blanket on the floor, or lie on the bed. Hands are as relaxed as possible.

If you are more comfortable sitting, then sit on a chair or pillow with a straight back and crossed legs.

Sit up straight, but without straining, so that your legs and body are comfortable.

2. Close your eyes and focus on your breathing.

Feel the air fill your body and leave it. Pay attention to the sensations that accompany movement air through the mouth, nose, throat and lungs.

Feel the chest and abdomen expand and fall as you breathe.

Concentrate on the places where the sensations in the body are strongest. Keep attention on every inhalation and exhalation. Just watch your breath without waiting for something special.

3. If you are distracted, gently return your attention back to the breath.

Try not to evaluate or criticize yourself. Our consciousness tends to be distracted, and the ability to notice that you are distracted, and returning attention to breathing is the basis of the practice meditation.

4. Your mind may or may not be calm.

Even if it's calm it is possible that it will be filled with thoughts or some kind of emotion. And these thoughts and emotions may also disappear soon. You may have different sensations in your body and this is also normal.

Whatever happens inside you, just watch the breath without reacting in any way, and without trying to change anything. Over and over, just return your attention to the breath.

5. Keep breathing. Keep watching.

Be in this practice for as long as you need.

6. After completing the meditation, pay attention to your condition and feelings. How are you feeling now? How comfortable are you? How helpful was this practice?

Meditation, like any new activity related to the development of the body and brain, often causes resistance. This is due to the increased energy expenditure, just like in a regular workout.

To make you want to continue meditation next time, you should not only understand its benefits with your mind, but also to experience it - this will be the main motivation for repeating sessions.

2. The practice of filling up with happiness

This practice will help you fill with positive emotions, cheer up and improve stress resistance.

It will help overcome negative tendencies of the mind, positively perceive yourself and look more optimistically at the world.

DURATION
For this practice, 4-5 minutes is enough.

REGULARITY
Do this practice 1-2 times a day.

Practice effect gradually accumulates and we become happier, stronger and kinder, both to ourselves and to those around us.

1. Get ready for practice.
Choose a quiet, comfortable place, sit comfortably (or you can lie down).
Close your eyes so that nothing outside distracts you from your practice.

2. Think back to any moment in your life when you were happy.
The moment you felt fulfilled, satisfied, and grateful. You can choose a time when you were completely protected, when you loved and were loved, when you achieved meaningful goals and received recognition - from yourself or from
other people. Or just when you were in a good place, with good people, and that's it.

3. Expand your memories.
What was the situation around, what could be observed from the place where you were?
What sounds were around you? Perhaps the voice of a loved one or the sounds of nature. Remember your sensations in the body. How relaxed were you then? What was your breath at that moment? Remember and relive the sensations on the skin. Maybe, the touch of hands or the warm rays of the sun, maybe it was a nice cool breeze.
Remember smells and collect small multiple experiences into a single, holistic experience.

4. Feel how your whole body and your mind is filled with this experience.
Feel how the happiness permeates all your cells and remains emotionally memory. Stay in this fullness for 10-20-30 seconds.

5. Connect your memories with reality.

Slowly open your eyes and combine your experience with the feeling of where you are now. Stay some more time with this experience. Thank life

for the fact that the experience of happiness is in your consciousness and in your memory, and, keeping it in yourself, smoothly move on to your daily activities and concerns. Bring this state of happiness in everything that you are going to do during the day.

3. Energizing the brain, body and senses

This morning practice actively activates the brain and gives our body bright sensory sensations. The best time and a place for her - morning wash and bathroom.

DURATION
This practice usually takes 5-10 minutes.

REGULARITY
Do the activation practice every morning for 1-2 weeks, then optional.

The practice of activating the brain, body and senses is based on three rules:
1. You do your usual activities with your eyes closed.
2. You act very carefully, paying attention to bodily sensations.
3. You observe your inner experiences and mark them by naming them to yourself.

After you have done the practice of awakening and attunement to values - close your eyes and try not to open them while doing your everyday morning routines. Imagine the path to the bathroom and try to walk it in your mind. Then slowly get up and try to walk this path for real.

If you have any difficulties, try to feel the space with your hands, make a few small steps and get your bearings. If that doesn't work, stop, open your eyes, look around, close your eyes and move on.

1. Go to the bathroom with your eyes closed and try to do everything that you do it normally, but with your eyes closed.
 Eyes can only be opened at the end practice when you leave the bathroom.
2. Pay attention to your body and how it feels.
3. Pay attention to your emotions.

The goal of this practice is not to be able to do everything right, the goal is to activate. When our vision is disabled (and this is one of the most important sensory systems), our brain tries to make up for the lack of information through memory, hearing, touch, and so on. It triggers brain activation.

The activation of the body is associated with an increase in the activity of touch and proprioception. Some of the most strong experiences with closed eyes - sensations on the surface of the body (touch) and signals from muscles inside the body (proprioception). Many people close their eyes intuitively, when swimming, in the shower, or at breakfast, enjoying the smell and taste of food.

Try, experiment and be careful, this exercise requires being very careful!

Your thoughts / notes

Chapter 5. Harmony. Life balance

You are the most important person in your life. Try to realise it.

You are always there for you. You should have love for yourself inside, you should care about yourself, you should make pleasant things and work on your spiritual development so that You feel better.

Your interception of life is manageable. The way you feel depends on how satisfied you are with the current life. Although, this satisfaction is not always justified. See, most of the people tend to expect more, all the time. It is in the human nature, we want something we cannot get right now, and worry because of one small thing, completely forgetting about all other things we already have and can be happy about.

Sometimes we take for granted things we always had, sometimes we get what we wanted and stop appreciating it the next day. That ruins harmony in life.

It is quite dangerous to always be unsatisfied with your current life, I should say to you. The reason I included this chapter to the books is that here I mostly talk about how to improve yourself, get closer and then reach your purposes and dreams, though there is one BUT. You should see a clear difference between a desire to become a better version of you, because you love yourself and want best, and constant attempts to change something because you are dissatisfied with yourself, your appearance, career and so on. That feeling can ruin you from inside. Basically, the difference is in perception and treatment to yourself here. Do you see this difference?

The motivation differs. to become better you, or to become somebody else, because you hate yourself.

When reaching goals, pursuing dreams, it is crucial to care about your feelings, notice when you are really tired and give yourself a rest, while still having discipline. You need to pay attention to the thoughts that fill your head, and be careful if most of them are negative.

A typical situation: you live and live, you think that you are on the right path, outwardly everything seems to be going quite successfully ... and suddenly one day you realize that you are not happy. What went wrong and when? It is likely that the fact is that you have never really listened to yourself and have a bad idea of your true self.

When we embody other people's ideas of success and happiness, when we do not hear our real voice, this leads to internal conflicts. It takes persistent effort to learn to differentiate between externally imposed goals and goals that are true for you personally. This effort will pay off. Because when you know how to listen to yourself, you make the right decisions for you personally and build the life you want. And this necessarily leads to a decrease in stress levels, increases self-esteem and brings satisfaction.

Steps that you can take :

1. Reflect on your values.

If you do not know your true values or accept other people's values for yours, you will experience anxiety and dissatisfaction. Look back at your life and remember what has ever brought you unconditional joy and enthusiasm?

For example, if you think money is valuable, then why do you hate your job as a financial planner, but are so happy to volunteer? Maybe it's really valuable for you not to receive, but to give?

The problem with basic beliefs is that until you are aware of them, they quietly rule you.

If you find it difficult to understand whether this is your value, imagine that your whole future life will be built exclusively around it. For example, you think power is valuable to you. Imagine that from now on you will only do what to give commands. Will you be happy? Or will you feel lonely? If the second option is correct, you may value leadership, not power.

2. Realize your basic beliefs.

These are your deepest ideas about the world, about other people, about yourself. It is quite possible that they were formed in childhood and inherited by you from other family members. For example, such as "The world is dangerous", "No one can be trusted", "Money is evil."

The problem with basic beliefs is that, until you become aware of them, they quietly rule you and influence all of your decisions. It is not easy to "get to the bottom" of them, it requires being extremely honest with yourself. Sometimes you need the help of a coach or counseling psychologist. But if you revisit the beliefs that drive you to wrong decisions and replace them with new ones that make your life easier, it will make an impressive difference.

3. Get to know your inner critic.

Listen to the voice in your head that, like a parent, tells you what to do. His tone makes you feel helpless and humiliated. This is not your true self, it is your inner critic. He speaks in the voice of a mother or father, mentor or teacher - someone who was stern and stern with you when you were growing up. Very often he uses the words "must", "must", "need". He also likes to compare you to others.

4. Break through the chaos.

One of the reasons why we cannot hear our true self is because we are overcome by many voices. It's like tuning in to one radio station when hundreds of them are on the air. In addition to the already mentioned inner critic, we can hear, for example, our inner child ("poor me, unhappy, no one loves me, no one appreciates what I do").

How to hear yourself in this polyphony? Try this writing technique. Take a pen and try to throw out your worries, discontent, anger, sadness, self-criticism on paper as quickly as possible, without caring about how it is written. It's a good way to break through the chaos to your true voice.

When you know how to be in the present moment, all worries and thoughts remain outside the brackets.

At first, it will be difficult to write even one or two sentences in which your real "I" will be felt, but when you practice, you can "call" it, barely touching the pen of the paper. Someone is more suited to another technique: not to write, but to say out loud everything that worries.

5. Practice daily.

Another extremely effective way to get over the word mixer in your head and hear yourself is through mindfulness practice, which is best done on a daily basis. When you know how to be in the present moment, all worries and thoughts remain outside the brackets.

6. Use your imagination.

If you only listen to your rational mind, you hear yourself only partially. Give free rein to your imagination - "what will happen if I ..." - and see what images and pictures your imagination draws.

7. Constantly ask yourself good questions.

Good questions are those that start with "What" and "How", not "Why". The fact is that the question "Why" often leads us to self-accusations, while "What" and "How" are aimed at the future and lead to new solutions.

Don't be afraid to ask yourself crazy big questions about the future, it will help you learn amazing things about yourself. Imagine what your ideal day would be if you were a multimillionaire? If you were to spend a week with your dream partner, what would you do? If you had only a week to live, how would you use that time?

8. Try something new once a week.

Many of us are confident that we know ourselves. But more often than not, we do what we were told about in childhood: this is good, it must be loved. Or what our parents did, what "all" our friends do.

The better we feel about ourselves, the better we understand ourselves. What can you do good for yourself this week?

Resist this "life of inertia" by doing something new, unusual for you once a week. Try some unusual exercise at the sports club or order an exotic, new meal at a restaurant. Talk to someone with whom you would never have thought of communicating. You will not like some of these innovations, and from time to time you will open some new facet in yourself.

9. Learn to let it go.

Holding on to what you have already outgrown means closing your access to your real self. This also applies to relationships. If you are surrounded by people with whom you have not had anything in common for a long time, and you communicate with them only because you have known each other since childhood, you interfere with your potential.

10. Take care of yourself! You, take care, of yourself.

The better we feel about ourselves, the better we understand ourselves. What can you do good for yourself this week? Maybe enjoy a fragrant bath instead of going to a boring event that is "inconvenient" to refuse? Or, finally, sit down and sort out your finances so you can stop worrying about them?

But if you are experiencing severe anxiety and therefore find it too difficult to hear yourself, consider the option of going to a psychologist or therapist. These experts know how to ask the right questions that will help you discover something about yourself that you never knew existed.

Actually, do not postpone your happiness for too long, the persvation you can refill it some time in the future is wrong.Do not postpone good things you can get today, for tomorrow.

Life balance and its impact on our happiness

I am pretty sure most of you have met successful career people who look like robots and make an impression of a totally unhappy working force, who do not notice anything around and are just concerned about productivity and money. You should have met a kind of people who haven't found their path in earning money as well - they tried a lot of things, but still cannot answer the question of what they want. You definitely have a friend of a friend - woman-housekeeper, who doesn't have anything in her life except cleaning, children' classes and cooking. Or a great guy who's always complaining he cannot find a right woman.

All these examples are people who haven't balanced their life. What I mean here is they have some aspects of their life which are fulfilled (or even overwhelmed with attention) , while others - missing.

Life balance is an interesting, active life according to its own rules, not a comfortable survival. To live exciting, you need to develop, try new things. Every day, be engaged in at least one or two activities that bring you joy. For me, a reliable source of joy is meaningful work.

You need to make a decision - to gradually regain control of your destiny. Learn to ride independently without external help on the wheel of the spheres of your life.

Look at the next page and find an example of Life Balance Wheel.

As you can see, this wheel has 8 sections, equally important for life filled with sense and happiness.
You will find an explanation of each section below.

1.   Health

Quality of food, sleep, presence of physical exercise, body state and healthy condition of all organs, absence of illness

2.   Work

The current level and speed of career development, the satisfaction from work and the desire to grow in that particular industry. Moderate loading by work, that leaves time for rest and leisure

3.   Social
•   The quality and quantity of friendship;
•   The broadness of network, both professional and social;community interaction;
•   Easiness to meet new people

4.   Development

Developing oneself as a person: mind, skills, knowledge, habits, character, reading books, learning languages and new things.

Cognition and development of oneself, as well as knowledge of the world, learning new things.

•   Personal growth - self-knowledge, culture, work on habits, the development of internal qualities, the achievement of personal perfection, the development of positive character traits;
•   Education - knowledge of the world, getting new skills, degrees, certificates, learning foreign languages

5.   Recreation

Recreation includes hobbies and passions, outdoor sports, massages, elements of self-care. Anything that involves getting rest and filling yourself with energy and resources would be considered recreation.

•   Hobbies
•   Quality of spare time
•   Fulfillment with energy and resources

6.   Family and Relationships

The quality of relationships with family and beloved ones, presence of support, care and love, level of commitment and involvement

7.   Life planning

How well the person understands what is likely to happen in 1, 2, 10 years, having plans and goals for the future.

8. Spirituality
- peace and harmony in life
- the ability to discover meaning and purpose in life
- understanding of values

Life Balance Wheel

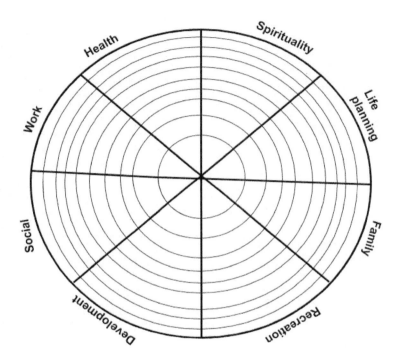

Assess the current state of each sphere from 1 to 10 points (1 - horror, 10 - everything is great). 1 - inside the circle, 10 - on the outside circle. As a result, you get the wheel of vital balance of your life.

Here I want to empathize that a happy person has a balance of these things. Continuous disregarding or failing to settle any of these aspects will eventually result in either anxiety, stress, bad mood, or feeling of waiting for life. Promise me, no way I want to scare you, I just want to explain the consequences and motivate you to pay attention here, and to fill your Life Balance Wheel.

The wheel of vital balance gives us an understanding of the state of each of the areas of our life. And accordingly, in which of the sectors we need to "work" in order to live a more fulfilling and harmonious life, to find happiness and desirable results.

It also helps us become more aware and responsible, and take control of our lives.

In order to live a full life, you need to comprehensively develop, learn new things, realize yourself and your potential. It is important to establish balance and harmony in general and reach new heights in each of the areas of your life.

Work on that persistently, and you notice how the quality of your life improves.

The "wheel of life" cannot be perfectly round - it is difficult to equally succeed in all desired areas. But it must be workable. Everyone has strengths, such as family support, bright talent or financial success, and they will become our support. But it is necessary to pay attention to sharp "failures". And the repair of our wheel should begin with those areas of life, positive changes which will help to cope with other problems. If your health fails, depriving you of the opportunity to work fully and to rest normally, we first deal with health. Not enough money for a house, a family, or entertainment? As a matter of priority, we are looking for how we will solve financial problems. But in order to change something in key areas, you need to change your attitude towards them, your very thinking, otherwise we will bury ourselves in the same ceiling that did not allow us to move on before. And here you need to make an effort and force yourself to be extremely honest with yourself. Remember that everything that you now think and write down for yourself - no one will see it, this is purely your analysis and your changes.

Here is my advice: have color pencils/markers with you, and fill each section of the life balance wheel with different colors, measuring your satisfaction in this sphere at this current stage of life from 0 to 10.

Dealing with limiting attitudes

We tend to ignore unpleasant facts - it's in our nature. And we do not just ignore them, but more often than not we refuse responsibility and blame the world around us for everything. It's easier to put up with what is happening. But the key is that if we do not make decisions on our own to cope with problems, we will remain hostages of the situation without the slightest opportunity to change anything in our life. Let's try to understand how this happens. Let's say we analyzed our health problems and realized that their cause is overweight. Surely he disturbed us before - so why didn't we do anything? It's all because of our limiting beliefs. To find them, write down all your thoughts about such a sad phenomenon on a piece of paper: "at my age, many are getting fat, and this is normal", "I just have such a metabolism", "I have neither the strength nor the time to go in for sports" ... What is the picture of all these statements? The circumstances are to blame, they are completely insurmountable from this point of view, which allows you to relieve yourself of responsibility. Now that we have said this to ourselves, we have two ways. The first is the "path of least resistance" - to leave everything as it is, exacerbating problems and degrading. The second is to make an informed decision, formulate a goal, break it down into stages and act.

Getting out of your daily rut, losing your usual stability is scary. But this is the only way to change life for the better. Even if it means, for example, the need to give up a bad habit, break off a painful relationship, leave an unloved job. It is not easy, but here we will be helped by the vision of our goal and the search for resources that can give us a sufficient amount of strength.

Draw your own image

On all the paths of self-improvement, we go to the real ourselves. Try to imagine yourself having achieved all your goals, what you will become after a while. What kind of person do I see myself as? How do I look? How do I feel? How do I realize myself in life? Where do I live? Who surrounds me? What place do close people take in my life? Of course, in some ways the fantasy will have to be tamed - it is impossible to become an opera singer without a voice. But a realistic, positive and inspiring picture will become a way for us to strive for, help us build a clear plan of goals and actions. It is important that such a picture really inspires, arouses admiration - "Wow, this is amazing! How wonderful I feel there! "

Each goal, ideally, should be specific, measurable and achievable over a certain period of time. Not "to lose a little weight", but "to lose 5 kilograms by June 1, and for this I need to reduce weight by about 500 grams per week". The fulfillment of such a goal does not seem incredible, will not deprive us of confidence and strength, and will give us joy at every stage, and when it is fully achieved. At the same time, it must be assumed that the road is not smooth, and success cannot be achieved without backtracking. There will be moments of weakness, loss of achieved intermediate results, moments of desire to give up everything and live as it turns out. This is totally normal. We fall, rise and move on. The general trend is important. It is this satisfaction, the feeling of a positive trend of change, increased self-esteem and self-love, improved health that are important, and not at all "spherical 90-60-90 in a vacuum". Then, at every step, a new resource appears that makes it possible to move on.

The chosen goals should be exactly ours, evoke your positive internal reaction, and not be achieved for our family or some "ideal person". This is our unique life, which should be a path not of stagnation and survival, but of development: full and joyful. It's difficult, especially in the beginning, but without a doubt the effort is worth it.

After it's done, look at the sections that have 0-5 scores. Write down these names of the sections in a notebook separately, and try to analyze what exactly is missing.

For example: you have "4" in the Development section. That probably means you are actually doing something already for your development, like reading motivational books, or learning to play guitar; but I guess you would like to work harder in that, or you see yourself developing in 2 directions, while actually working just in 1 of them.

I had such a situation in my 20's. I was working hard on professional development, and learning foreign language, still not ranking my development as "8-10", but "5", since I wanted to draw and do swimming as well. Just didn't have time for all these activities.

So here is another question: how well your priorities are set and do you know the direction you are following.

It is easy to be dissatisfied with your life, it is harder to figure out why.

Do that. Think deep, hardly every person has an aspect where he/she is not satisfied with a current result. Find out reasons.

Then, your task is to think how, and when! you can improve the situation. Again, here we are analyzing each section separately. So if you had 0-5 in Work, Development, and Social — you are writing down your expectations and worries about each of it, and you are solving a task of how you can change it separately as well.

It's crucial for you to determine the things you can fix right away, and the problems you are not able to influence right now.

To realize your intentions of fixing the first type of things - you'll need self-control and persistence, planning and being strict to yourself (caring about the feelings still).

Now the task is not to miss problems you cannot influence right away. You NEED to define for yourself When and How you are changing it. You need to have a Plan. For each section, for each issue.

That is a time-consuming and responsible task. I encourage you to choose an evening/day, when nobody can disturb you. Like 2-3 hours of silence and calm atmosphere. You need to focus your mind and look inside your soul. That's an amazing practice to find out both your satisfaction from your current life, And imagination of a better life, better you.

If you do it properly, you definitely will receive a couple of new purposes you haven't even thought about. That is wonderful. It means your unconsciousness will come out on the paper.

So, let's say you have analyzed aspects separately, found out reasons of imbalance and got your ways to solve it, separately.

Now the task is to combine these strategies and ideas from different life aspects into one united plan of actions. We are making a guide for you to move to a better life. While it's done - you are having a role of performer, following guidelines made by yourself.

Why is that important? A human being is not able to think about and control all aspects of life at the same time. Especially when routine tasks deadlines are coming closer, the weather is bad etc. We have to fix on paper our treatment to life and expectations while being in the best state of mind and feelings, make a PLAN, and follow it no matter what. To do this, we need to have an exact requirement for every month, week, and day. Again, you cannot work on every single problem at the same time, but you Can choose a day of an hour for every exact issue.

Here we come closer to time management and life planning.

Why?

See, making up ideas about what you want and what you need is not an end point. Now we need to realize your purposes. How ?

Again, everything depends on you. Just knowing the technique and writing down plans won't make them come true. Just actions do that.

To make these actions organized, and not to make you overwhelmed with the purposes, we need to give your brain an exact task every day. Small task. Split big purposes into smaller parts. Taking into account your time, abilities and obstacles.

Sometimes you don't have enough information on how to get from point A to point B. Let's say you always wanted to be a web-designer, while working as an accountant for some building company. So you have that in mind and do not enjoy your current life because of this idea. But you have never searched for the ways to become a web-designer. You know your "why I can't", and do not "waste" time in looking for opportunities.

What should this abstract woman I described above do? Well, first of all, look at the situation realistic. Staying at the previous job and doing the same actions will in no way bring her to a nice office or freelance work of web-designer. What will?

1.   Searching for opportunities to learn the skills required for that exact profession (courses, YouTube videos, a friend who has been working in that area as a source of information etc) — so she needs to have an instrument

2.   Estimation of time during normal week that she can spend on getting new skills (pay attention: I am not saying she should quit her job right after realizing she can't live without web design. It's a possible way for people who have some money savings and can afford not to earn salary for 3-6 months)

So we have an answer to a question "how", and "when".

Now I'd recommend to

3. Test a dream

What I mean is to spend up to 20 hours doing what you think you want to be doing.

Sometimes people imagine a great picture of being somebody else/doing different things in the daily routine, and completely exclude negative moments or difficulties that activity may include.

I once read an example of a middle-aged woman, who had this intrusive "dream" to work laying under the palms. She lived in the industrial city and saw plms before just on vacations for a week or so before. When she was thinking about working on a sunbed under the palms, a beautiful picture from a different world appeared to her: perfect air temperature, sunny day, she lays in her swimsuit and does some pleasant easy things in her laptop, then drinks a cocktail and runs into the water. She was so obsessed with that image, that she almost quit her job in the industrial city. Then her friend offered her a deal, which meant she would take a long vacation for a month, and go to her miracle beach, still working (but on her own project, not for the firm). If everything goes well and she actually enjoys that type of life, - she would quit her job, sell the flat and go live on the shore.

What do you think has happened in a week? Our character quickly missed her colleagues, office atmosphere and having a separation of working hours and place - and the rest ones. She felt unstable and worried, not being able to see any future perspectives and opportunities, like being cut out from the rest of the world. She realised what she actually wanted was coming to the shore twice per year and spending there 2 weeks, to fill herself with sun, salt water and have such a place just for the rest. She still wanted the benefits of city life, comfort and understanding what is gonna happen in 5 years.

Imagine what would happen if she actually quit the job and sold the flat?

Of course, there are multiple examples of happy end stories when people quit office jobs one day and go live their perfect life from dreams. But such stories mostly miss the ways the people overcome, just mentioning happy consequences. That is misleading!

I want you to be aware of that, and make a decision about changing some aspect of your life, taking all responsibility and realising the risks and coming challenges. When that is okay, I definitely encourage you to work hard towards getting what you really want!

4. When you see you really are able to do what you thought you wanted, and you are getting more motivation + you have a better idea how to, let's say make a simple website design, you can move to a 2-3 month planning on how to develop in that direction

If we continue with an example of an accountant/web-designer, after 1 month theoretical learning and repeating practical tasks, she can tell her friends she now learns web-design and suggest making it for free — creating a portfolio. The other way is to register on freelance websites and take orders for a small price - to get reviews and cases for the portfolio.

All of those things should be done in a special time during the week - defined before.

After starting earning up to half of the salary on a new profession — you can safely quit and find a job there.

That is just one example, showing "how". It's all individual. The main point is persistency, and actions with a plan.

Use the techniques of time-management stated in Chapter 7 to do a better job in making your dreams (=goals) come true!

Your thoughts / notes

Chapter 6. Making smart plans

Making plans and seeing where you are going is an important part of moving forward, professional and personal development.

To do that better, I offer you following particular rules and advice, based on my personal and other people's experience. There are multiple techniques that work in different mechanisms. I'll offer the ones that work together and are effective for most of the people (when acting, not just planning ;))

After reading Chapter 5 and doing exercises/practices provided there, you should have quite a clear understanding of what you want from life now, and some ideas on how to get there. This chapter is intended to give you an instrument.

1.   Sit down and write purposes from the life balance wheel for the next Year. That will give you an understanding of what direction you are moving in. Do not overestimate yourself, try to be objective, still ambitious.

2.   Now define purposes for the next month. Purposes for the year should give you direction and 3-5 spheres you are developing in.

If your purpose for the year says "Learn how to dance contemporary", the purpose for the month might be "find a dance school, and take the first lesson, get equipment". If your year's purpose states "learn German to B1", the monthly purpose might be "find a language school/a tutor, get books, and learn tenses, vocabulary for school/public transport/ travel vocabulary ".

Basically, you should divide big purposes into 12 parts, and follow it every month. It would work for a gradual purpose like learning a new language, although it wouldn't work for some goals like "try scuba-diving". That is okay, that type of goal should be planned in advance, and you do not need to work the whole year for that. It might involve saving money though, that would influence your monthly budget planning.

3.   When we have a plan for the month, it's time to learn planning the week.

That task is fairly easier since it mostly involves routine deals, not long-term planning. What I recommend is using paper planners for that. For sure, you can use digital planners, apps, or google calendar. Although, writing down tasks for each day of the week on Sunday would serve as a ritual to get ready and put you in a mood of pursuing purposes. That is why I recommend beginners in planning to use paper planners.

When you are making a week plan, you should not write every single thing you are gonna do each day. Your task is to put the appointments, meetings, classes to your planner that have an exact time, plus mention important things that should be done during each day.

4.   When planning each day in the evening before, you can basically write what you do and at what time, using the order. You do not need to do that every single day, although if your day seems to be busy and you are trying to realize which order of tasks is better, and if you are able to fit one more task, it's better to write timing too.

I want to introduce you to the technique "**Getting things done**" made by David Allen.

David Allen recommends abandoning the classic rigid day scheduling, when the entire day is scheduled in minutes. This kind of planning is rarely practical because you can be distracted at any time and plans can change.

David believes that tasks are tough and flexible.

Flexible tasks follow a simple list. These are tasks that can be completed at any given time, so they can be completed in order. Most of the tasks of the average person fall into this category.

Hard tasks are tasks that are tied to a specific time. For example, a meeting, conference, scheduled call, task is due to expire.

It makes sense to leave only tough tasks on the calendar. At the start of the day, you view your calendar list and task list. It is most convenient when the task list and calendar are on the same page. It's easier to plan this way. If at the beginning of the day there are no tough things planned, then you can perform flexible tasks in order: depending on the availability of time, energy and resources, you perform tasks from highest priority to lowest priority. As soon as it's time for a hard task, you interrupt, perform a hard task, and then return to performing tasks on the list. This is the most flexible, simple and convenient way of planning when dealing with a large number of cases.

There are also more modern tools that help to work according to the GTD methodology - these are electronic organizers. If the organizer allows you to create a list of tasks, sort tasks in the list in any order, divide tasks into folders (or contexts, categories, kairos, tags, which is the same thing), keep a calendar.

Immediately after the book became popular, many programs appeared on the computer that allow you to work according to the GTD method. The problem with planning both with paper and trays and with the help of programs on a computer is that a modern specialist often does not care where he is. He can do his job at home, in the office or in Thailand.

In addition to the fact that the online organizer TimeMaster has all the capabilities to work according to the GTD method, information is available to you from home, office and anywhere in the world.

David also mentions top-down planning in his book. He uses the analogy of reviewing goals, projects and tasks "from the height of flight":

1. current affairs;

2. current projects;

3. terms of reference;

4. the coming years (1-2 years);

5. five-year perspective (3-5 years);

6. life.

Estimation method
Often in the planning process, important tasks get lost among minor tasks. This is because we do not mark their priority. Even if you understand the need to complete a task, it is important to state it in writing. Indeed, during the working day, there is not always time to adequately assess the importance of each case.

How it works
Give the planned tasks points from zero to two, depending on the degree of importance. The main priority is two points. The one point task can be completed later. Small responsibilities and daily tasks get zero points.

Remember to rate the work at the end of the day, for example on a five-point scale. An unfulfilled business, which received 1 or 2, will affect the upcoming work and cause inconvenience. Like bad grades in school. This is important for understanding your own performance and managing your schedule.

Method 1-3-5

A large number of cases discourage the desire to take on them. Therefore, many time management experts advise to single out up to nine tasks and perform them depending on the degree of importance.

So, minor goals can be transferred to another day, while completing the most important of the planned tasks. Method 1–3–5 is fairly easy to use, although it takes some time and effort to isolate tasks.

How it works

Plan nine things for yourself every day: 1 - the most important task, will always be in priority; 3 - cases that require resolution during the working day; 5 - small tasks that are performed whenever possible.

Do not forget that you need to keep the number of cases and not exceed it. Otherwise, the method will be ineffective.

Card method

This planning method was proposed by the famous Russian time management specialist Gleb Arkhangelsky. He provides business training, writes books, and even runs his own time management consulting company. Along with some principles, Gleb also developed a method for quick planning using cards.

How it works

A thick diary is not needed in this case: just a few sheets of paper are enough. Get three cards for different purposes. They can be multi-colored, marked or with stickers. The main thing is that they differ from one another and, of course, you like them.

The first card is strategic. It will contain your key goals, to achieve which you need to make every possible effort. In the second, devoted to long-term goals, you write down all the activities and plans for the year or several years ahead. The third card will contain the most important event of the upcoming day. And it will, of course, change most often.

Lifetime realizing

That is a good method of rather philosophical thinking and realizing how quickly life passes by, to remove doubtful purposes from your list, and devote time to actually important things.

Here is what you need to do: you take a squared notebook, get one piece of paper, and fill with colour every cell as every month of your life by that current time.

Each line is a year of your life. The table is approximate and we take 75 years as a standard lifetime.

Try doing that and leave that on the wall / on the table as a reminder about the time limit all of us get. Would be great if you filled one more cell every month after.

Your thoughts / notes

Chapter 7. Gratitude

Let's start with a definition of gratitude. In a nutshell if something turns out to be useful for us, we can evaluate it with our positive thoughts, words, actions in response.This reaction is called gratitude. So we declare: "I am very glad that you were useful to me."

Why should you be grateful?
First of all, this is the only way to appreciate life and everything that is in it. There is no other way to appreciate it.

When you thank a person, you let him know that he was useful to you, and you appreciated what he did for you. When you thank fate, the Universe, God, good luck for something, you make it clear to the world that this is important to you. What is even more important, you remind Yourself that it's something meaningful and great, so that you pay attention and do not take it for granted.

The principle is pretty simple: when you value what you have, it speaks of your maturity, of your responsibility. Usually such a person gets even more over time. And those who do not value get nothing. For reference, this mechanism is governed by the law of universe equilibrium.

Let me explain why nature does not like ungrateful people so much. Imagine that you have a very expensive diamond and you temporarily need to deposit it. You are unlikely to entrust it to someone who does not understand the true value of a gem. You will choose a responsible person who understands jewelry or at least approximately knows how special and rare it is. Such a person simply cannot disregard your request to look after the stone.

In life the system works mostly the same, with the only exception that here The Universe has "a diamond" and decides who to give it to (or God, or a higher mind, or energy, or nature - the essence does not change from the name, the name depends only on what is easier for you to understand). Instead of a precious stone, a huge resource is concentrated in her hands in the form of material and intangible wealth, various capabilities, human qualities, a variety of circumstances and others. Everything that we can have in our life is in the hands of the Universe.

Just as your stone is dear to you, the Universe values its unlimited resources.
The universe needs to somehow distribute them in such a way that they are all involved. There are human beings who can potentially work with these resources.

People are divided into two categories: grateful and ungrateful. After all, what gratitude is - you clearly understand how much value falls to you, so you use your resources very carefully and appreciate your abilities, skills and potential.

Gratitude is a universal remedy for any ailment. If you are grateful, you cannot be a pessimist in any way, you cannot be evil or selfish as well. The feeling of gratitude always crowds out unnecessary things over time, so a grateful person is more positive and optimistic (and if not, then over time he becomes such).

If gratitude did not exist, then we would not do anything for each other, because the meaning of our actions in relation to others would be lost. Doing something about a person that gratitude bursts him from the inside, you begin to treat yourself differently. By these actions we are trying to show and understand ourselves, to answer the question "who am I ?!"

How to be grateful
Before thinking about how to be grateful, you need to assess how grateful you are now. This is easy enough to understand. Ungrateful people are often offended by life and constantly upset about what happens to them, they are rarely satisfied with themselves and often complain about injustice.

Only observant people know how to say "thank you". Therefore, take your eyes off the floor and look at the world around you. We always have something to be grateful for, and this list is quite long. To begin with, we have a life, you can be grateful to everything until the end of days just for this. Because everyone around us has life, it never ceases to be the greatest gift.

Each person has so many opportunities to reveal his potential, an infinity of different activities, people, circumstances, feelings.

The world around us is so multifaceted! Our trouble is that we have become accustomed to, have become absent-minded observers and have ceased to notice the miracles around.

Whether you are grateful or not, here are two simple exercises. They won't take long in your busy schedule, but the result will be amazing if you do them right.

Practice. Letter of gratitude

So let's write a letter of thanks. It should take into account everything that you can say "thank you" for in your life, from the essential things to the little things like a hot shower or a cool shirt.

You can start with the words "I am grateful that I have a life." You can address someone specifically (including yourself), for example: "Thank you, mom, for being so kind." Thank you for everything: people, circumstances, material things, your qualities, nature, appearance, negativity, and so on. Try to explain what exactly you are grateful for, concerning a thing, person, circumstance. Make the letter as complete and comprehensive as possible so that there is nothing to add.

Re-read your essay once a month, and if you see that you can add, then be sure to add it with the date.

An indicator of effective adherence to instructions is a gradual increase in the volume of writing, which indicates the development of observation.

Twice a week, you need to find a few minutes when you have the time and desire to work out.

Your task is to thank for all the positive and negative things that happened to you over the past week. Do not deceive yourself with phrases like: "This time I have nothing to say." Even if the world is about to end, there are at least 10 reasons why you could express your gratitude over the past three days.

It is important not to turn the execution of the instruction into a simple pronunciation of the memorized text. It would be good to feel joy when you thank, then the text will be born by itself, and you won't have to invent it. Feelings of joy and warmth, by the way, are the main indicator of following the instructions correctly.

Don't thank if you don't want to. It is very important here to experience positive emotions in the process, if this cannot be achieved today, then you do not need to force yourself.

Don't stop at just twice a week. After a while, people come to this point on their own, if they do everything right.

Don't automatically say: "thank you". We have all already formed a mindset that allows us to simply say words without attaching importance to them.

Gratitude should be a conscious action.

I hope you now understand the importance of learning how to be grateful.

One more thing I want to mention in this chapter is the equivalence of happiness and gratitude.

Happiness has a bad memory. It appears in "now", because it forgets what happened yesterday, and does not want to think about what will happen tomorrow.

To be happy now, you should always keep in mind great moments of the past few days/weeks, and feel gratitude for that. If you follow that advice, your heart will be filled with positive emotions, and your mind - with positive thoughts.

That is a simple, but very powerful instrument.

Good luck!

Your thoughts / notes

Chapter 8. The better you

This chapter will bring you to the understanding of what life you want to have,
how you imagine "perfect you", and how to get there.
Before that, let's take 5 minutes and make a small practice here.

What do you fantasize about when you look out the train window before going
to bed or when you pretend to listen to a boring person hanging noodles on your ears?
Are you standing on the comedy club stage in front of thousands of hysterical fans?
Or are you surrounded by beautiful children in the coziest and happiest house in the
world? Or are you celebrated for setting up orphanages around the globe? Do this
exercise as if money is not a problem.

Have you ever caught yourself thinking: "That is not me. I do not want to be
like that. I do not want to be here. I want a better life."? Have you ever been
dissatisfied with what you have, but still doing nothing to fix that?

Here is the thought -- maybe you don't do anything to improve your "now",
because you don't understand clearly Where you want to be. One more reason could
be the fact that you know, but somehow you think you cannot make it, you are not that
type of person who can live such a life.

Let me tell you something here. You Can. He who thinks he can and he who
thinks he can't -- are both equally right. Remember? That's you who decides.

Repeat that to yourself. I CAN. If I want to. If I need it. I decide what life I
have. I am responsible for my "now" and "tomorrow". I cannot change the past, but I
definitely can choose the future.

"He who says he can and he who says he can't - are both equally right"
Will Smith

It is really important to know how to abstract from your current life and look at
it in a different way, after planning, making actions and being busy all the time. You
can get used to some kind of ritual, like going out of the city each month for the
weekend, and analysing what happened before.

I actually strongly recommend this method, as going out of your daily routine
allows your brain to get new ideas, take a rest and notice details. See, when we are
doing the same things day to day, using the same routes, the same car, living in the
same house for several years -- we stop noticing what is around. We do not see the
trees, we do not know what colour of curtains are in our bedroom, what we were
wearing yesterday, and cannot describe what food we ate 3 days ago. It is natural for

our brain to process repeated information on the back, without the presence of consciousness. That is wise at some point : we do not get actually involved in many processes and can think about some work project on the way home. But! When that happens all the time, we live in an automatic mode and need to learn how to consciously take ourselves out of it to see life.

So how do we do that?

Step aside and look at your life, imagining that's the life of somebody else, - is the best proven method. Your task is to analyse would you be satisfied with your life if you could (for some reason) change the current life. In other words, what would you think about a person having a very similar life to your own?

Would you have some advice for him? Would you feel sorry? Or amazed?

Would you be jealous or angry?

Try to focus on that for a couple of minutes, and do not lie to yourself answering the question. Keep that conclusion to yourself, and then try to find out reasons for the feeling you got.

Why? What aspect of that life, or what factor made an impact? What exactly would you like to change there? Is it even possible? Theoretically.

If it is, why haven't you changed that yet? Why?

Answer to yourself. Accept the fact you haven't done anything yet.

I have an amazing practice you can try on you, but you would better have help from your friend /relative / beloved one. That is a game called **"Grand vision".**

Here are the rules: there is one dreamer, and one moderator. Dreamer sits comfy/lays down, relaxes, closes eyes and listens to the voice of the moderator.

Moderator starts talking and does that slowly, calmly and makes pauses after each frase. Dreamer does not answer his questions loud, just in his head.

- Imagine your best self in 10 years
- You wake up
- What time is it? Did you wake up yourself, or someone/something woke you up?
- Where are you? Look out and describe the room, try to focus on details
- Did you wake up alone?
- Look outside through the window, what is there? Do you know the exact place where you are? Country, city, district?
- Go to the mirror
- What do you see? What does your hair look like? Face? Body? What are you wearing?
- Okay, what would you do next? Try to describe the morning
- What are you doing next? What plans do you have? How do you feel?

- Where would you spend the day? Who would you see?
- What are you eating for lunch? Where?
- Where do you go in the afternoon?
- Would you cook dinner, or go to have it somewhere?
- What would you wear?
- How would you like to spend the evening? What would you think about before sleep?
- Open your eyes

After being in that state I strongly recommend to write down the day you imagined, and describe with as many details as possible. If you get any thoughts in the process of writing, note them too.

That is who you want to be. My congratulations.

I have good news now. You still can influence the situation and be that person. Find the ways to do that. But, please, do not leave that task for later, for the evening, for the weekend. We tend to postpone important things, postponing for days, months, years! All you need to do -- is to analyse right. now.

Your thoughts / notes

.. Epilogue

Your task is to find the courage to create the brightest, happiest, and coolest version of yourself.

The good news is this is possible.
We must first move from the stage of wanting a better life to the decision to change it.
And then take the first step.
And then the second one.

The bad news is that no one else can do it. You must do it yourself.

You will probably have to do what you never imagined before. What an experience! What an expansion of the worldview! And how hard!

You have to believe in something that cannot be seen, but it definitely exists.

All these cool things, wonderful experiences, exciting events are already here, next to you. They are patiently waiting for you to join the common holiday. And the only thing it takes from you is to go and get it.
So go, and get it!

Conclusions from reading the book

_____
_____
_____
_____
_____
_____
_____
_____
_____
_____
_____
_____
_____
_____
_____
_____
_____
_____
_____
_____
_____
_____
_____
_____
_____
_____
_____
_____

Disclaimer

This book contains opinions and ideas of the author and is meant to teach the reader informative and helpful knowledge while due care should be taken by the user in the application of the information provided. The instructions and strategies are possibly not right for every reader and there is no guarantee that they work for everyone. Using this book and implementing the information therein contained is explicitly your own responsibility and risk. This work with all its contents, does not guarantee correctness, completion, quality or correctness of the provided information. Misinformation or misprints cannot be completely eliminated. Human mistake is real!

Printed in Great Britain
by Amazon